Liam The Dreamer

Written by Yvette Daniels
Words edited by Melissa Colgan
Words edited by Shelia Y. Darden

Illustrated by: Tooba Imtiaz

This Book Belongs to:

_____

Thank you to

Pastor Derrick Lindsey
Terry Wilson
Micah Jackson

For being an encouragement to African American Boys, Pre-Teens, Teenagers, Young Adult Males and Men. Thank you for taking the time to pray, write a prayer, and provide words of encouragement that will impact their lives and having a desire to see them flourish in the things of God.

Hello, my name is Liam, The Dreamer. I love to dream. I dream about everything. My mom told me she gave me the nickname Dreamer because she had the most amazing dreams about me before I was born.

I am always wondering and thinking about what I am going to be when I grow up.
Even though I am little, I can still dream. You are never too little to dream. Before I go to bed, I pray and ask God to give me good dreams.

I dreamed I was a Superhero; I was helping a child who was stuck in the tree.

I dreamed I was a Dentist; I was fixing someone's teeth.

I dreamed I was a Music Teacher; I was standing in front of a class – conducting a band.

I dreamed I was a Doctor;
I was in a hospital and doing surgery on a patient.

I dreamed I was a Scientist;
working in a research lab.

I dreamed I was a Businessman; working in an office.

One day I said, "I do not want to dream anymore."

My mom asked me why and I told her what happened. We were having a shared day in our class - this is the day when you get to share about things in your life. I shared with my class about my dreams, when I grow up and get big. They laughed at me and said, "you can't do that." I was so sad. I told my teacher I do not want to share anymore. My teacher talked to the class about being respectful and not laughing at anyone in the class. Even so, I still do not want to share or dream anymore.

My mom said, "Dreamer, why do you think I gave you the nickname Dreamer?" I know in my heart you will be somebody one day. So, I need you to keep dreaming. Everywhere you go in life someone is not going to like what you say or do. However, you cannot let that stop you. People have their own fears and insecurities about themselves. Sometimes other children do not have anyone to encourage them to dream. So, I need you to keep dreaming.

"Ok," said Dreamer, "I will keep dreaming." So, that night before I went to bed, I prayed and asked God to give me sweet dreams again. Wow, that night, I had 4 dreams about what I could do.

I dreamed I was a Firefighter;

I was putting out a fire in a building.

I dreamed I was Lawyer;

I was in the courtroom helping people.

I dreamed I was a Judge;

making good and right decisions.

I dreamed I was a Preacher;
preaching at church.

When I woke up in the morning, I told my mom I had 4 dreams that night. She said to me, "keep dreaming, son." You can be all you want to be. Just stay focused and do not allow anyone to tell you what you can and cannot do. When you grow up, you can choose what is the best fit for your life.

Scriptures

NIV – New International Version
KJV – King James Version
NLT – New Living Translation

Jeremiah 29:11 (KJV)

For I know the thoughts that I think toward you, saith the LORD, thoughts of peace, and not of evil, to give you an expected end.

Philippians 4:13 (KJV)

I can do all things through Christ which strengtheneth me.

1 Peter 2:9 (KJV)

But ye are a chosen generation, a royal priesthood, an holy nation, a peculiar people; that ye should shew forth the praises of him who hath called you out of darkness into his marvellous light.

Psalms 139:14 (KJV)

I will praise thee; for I am fearfully and wonderfully made: marvellous are thy works; and that my soul knoweth right well.

Isaiah 55:11 (KJV)

So shall my word be that goeth forth out of my mouth: it shall not return unto me void, but it shall accomplish that which I please, and it shall prosper in the thing whereto I sent it.

2 Corinthians 9:8 (NLT)

And God will generously provide all you need. Then you will always have everything you need and plenty left over to share with others.

Joshua 1:9 (NLT)

This is my command—be strong and courageous! Do not be afraid or discouraged. For the LORD your God is with you wherever you go."

2 Timothy 1:7 (KJV)

For God hath not given us the spirit of fear; but of power, and of love, and of a sound mind.

Prayers

Father God, I thank you for all the Dreamers in the world. I pray for an extra hedge of protection over them. Lord, I pray that you will keep them from all hurt, harm, and danger. Lord, I pray they will do good in school. I pray they will be good readers and writers. I pray that they will hear your voice early in life and for the direction of their life. I bind every negative word that has been spoken over them and to them. I pray that your will and your way be done in their life in Jesus' name,
Amen!

Father, I pray for this little dreamer. I pray that he will always acknowledge you in all of his ways. I pray that his dreams would be more than self-serving...that they would be dreams of helping others. I pray that he will never give up...that he will always know that You are for him...that he will always have real friends that would never look to take advantage of him. I pray that his life would be a light to his peers, and that he would remember You in the days of his youth. In Jesus' name...
Amen!

May the God of our Lord Jesus, the Father of Glory give you Dreams and Visions. God, we thank you for revealing to _____ (insert name) the reason(s) that you brought him to this Earth. Fill _____ with the inspiration, strategies and stick-to-it-ness needed to bring these dreams and visions to reality. May _____ be humbled yet honored that you have chosen him for a time like this.
Amen.

Prayers for Boys

Father God, we pray for ____ (insert name) and for all young men like him, will come to know that they are fearfully and wonderfully made (Psalms 139:13-16) by a loving God. I thank you Lord that you created _____, you designed him to look exactly like the person that we see today. Lord, from the shape of _____ eyes, the color of his skin, to his exact height and weight, you created ____ for a purpose, you knew ____ while he was in his mother's womb/tummy/stomach. We pray that ____ will always know that he was not born by mistake, that God created him for a purpose. I thank you Lord that _____, like all of us, was created because of the Love that God has for us. And that through God's Son, Jesus Christ, we are created do good works and to share God's love and not to do evil.

I thank you Lord, that your WORD says "No Weapon formed against us shall succeed." That means that ____ can trust you to protect him from hurt, harm, and danger. That also means that the Lord will protect all of us from giving in to bad influences and other temptations. I thank you God that ____ will come to know Jesus Christ as his Lord and Savior. I pray that ____ will come to know you as a Friend (John 15:13), as a Protector (Psalm 3:3), as a Savior (Jeremiah 39:17-18), and as a Father (John 14:6). Lord, we know that no one's life is perfect, as a result, we all need to have a relationship with you, we need to know you. So, Lord, I pray that you're sending help ____ way. And that as long as he seeks through prayer and reading your written Word (Philippians 4:6-7) each day, that you will send people (as true friends, protectors, spiritual fathers) into ____ life that will help be assets to his life and not liabilities.

So, Lord, I pray in accordance with (2 Timothy 1:7) that ____ no longer has to be afraid. No longer has to live in fear. No longer feel as if he is alone, because you are with him. I thank you, Lord that you are releasing your power, your love, your peace, and self-control in ____ life. And in accordance with Numbers 6:24-26, I thank you for what you have done, are doing, and will do in ____ life. In Jesus' name, we pray, Amen!

African American Men Dreamers

Dr. Martin Luther King, Jr.

Jesse Owens

George Washington Carver

Edward Bouchet

Michael Jordan

Kobe Bryant

Tyler Perry

Chadwick Boseman

Idris Elba

Lance Gross

Michael B. Jordan

Denzel Washington

Miles Brown

LeBron James

Shaquille O'Neal

And many more....

"If You Dream It, You Can Be It"
"Dreamers Make a Difference"

Daily Affirmations

I am Strong!

I am Bold!

I am Smart!

I am Intelligent!

I am Handsome!

I am Loved!

I Love who I Am!

I am Brave!

I am Safe in the Arms of God!

I am a Good Listener!

Failure is not a part of my Life!

I am not afraid of any Challenges!

I can say "NO" if it is not Comfortable for me!

I will use Kind Words!

I can do all things through Christ!

About The Author

Yvette Daniels comes from a large family of Singers and Musicians. She is a Musician, Music Teacher, and Minister of Worship at her church. Yvette has been teaching music for over 20 years. Yvette has published 8 Children's Books and 8 Coloring and Activity Books. She has also published a Christian Book – Breaking Free (Freedom From the Snares). Yvette is currently in the process of completing 2 more Children's Books and a Songbook.

CHILDREN BOOKS AVAILABLE BY
YVETTE DANIELS

Amazon & Barnes & Nobles

Harry, Harry, the Dancing Hippo

Ten Singing Cockatiels

Dance, Jump, Hop and Sing

The Music on the Bus

Sweet Pea Paw Prints

Liberty Beautiful Hair

Unicorn Coloring Book

African American Magic Coloring Book

African American Black Girls Coloring Book

Monster Truck Coloring Book

Animal Dot to Dot Coloring Book

African American Coloring Book

Brown Girls Princess Coloring Book

The Dreamers (for Girls)

Email: victoriousfruit@hotmail.com

Seven Little Mice Chasing Waves

Bubbles the Goldfish Coloring and Activity Book

Breaking Free (Freedom From the Snares)

www.ingramcontent.com/pod-product-compliance
Lightning Source LLC
Chambersburg PA
CBHW042017090426
42811CB00015B/1669